THE FACSIMILE TEXT SOCIETY

SERIES III: PHILOSOPHY

VOLUME 2

RALPH CUDWORTH

A SERMON

1647

Sole British Agents,
B. H. BLACKWELL, LTD.,
50 & 51 Broad Street,
Oxford, England.

RALPH CUDWORTH

A SERMON

PREACHED BEFORE THE HOUSE OF COMMONS
MARCH 31, 1647

Reproduced from the Original Edition

THE FACSIMILE TEXT SOCIETY

NEW YORK

1930

Printed in the United States of America
by The National Process Company, New York

BIBLIOGRAPHICAL NOTE

A Sermon Preached before the Honourable House of Commons, At Westminster, March 31, 1647, by Ralph Cudworth is reproduced from a copy of the original edition in the library of Union Theological Seminary; this copy has been compared with another copy of the same edition in the same library, and no variations have been found.

F.A.P.

Columbia University
　July 15, 1930

A
SERMON

Preached before the Honourable House of

COMMONS,

At
WESTMINSTER,
March 31. 1647.

By R. Cudworth, B. D.

Εὐσέβει ὦ τέκνον· ὁ γὰρ Εὐσεβῶν ἄκρως Χριστιανίζει.

CAMBRIDGE.

Printed by *Roger Daniel*, Printer to the
University.
1647.

To
THE HONOURABLE
House of
COMMONS.

He Scope of this Sermon, which not long since exercised your Patience (Worthy Senatours) was not to contend for this or that Opinion; but onely to perswade men to the Life of Christ, *as the Pith and Kernel of all Religion. Without Which, I may boldly say, all the severall Forms of Religion in the World, though we please our selves never so much in them, are but so many severall* Dreams. *And those many Opinions about Religion, that are every where so ea-*

gerly

gerly contended for on all sides, where This *doth not lie at the* Bottome, *are but so many* Shadows *fighting with one another: so that I may well say, of the true Christian, that is indeed possessed of the Life of Christianity, in opposition to all those that are but lightly tinctured with the Opinions of it, in the language of the* Poet,

Οἷος πέπνυται τοὶ δ' ὡς σκιαὶ ἀΐσσυσι.

Wherefore I could not think any thing else, either more Necessary for Christians in generall, or more Seasonable at this time, then to stirre them up to the reall Establishment of the Righteousnesse *of* God *in their hearts, and that* Participation *of the* Divine Nature, *which the* Apostle *speaketh of. That so they might not content themselves, with mere* Phancies *and* Conceits *of* Christ, *without the* Spirit *of* Christ *really dwelling in them, and* Christ *himself inwardly* formed *in their hearts. Nor satisfie themselves, with the mere holding of right and* Orthodox Opinions, *as they conceive; whilest they are utterly devoid within of that* Divine Life, *which* Christ *came to kindle in mens Souls; and therefore are so apt to spend all their zeal upon a violent obtruding of their own* Opinions *and* Apprehensions *upon others, which cannot give entertainment*

tainment to them: which, besides its repugnancy to the Doctrine and Example of Christ himself, is like to be the Bellows, that will blow a perpetuall Fire of Discord and Contention, in Christian Commonwealths: whilest in the mean time, these hungry, and starved Opinions, devoure all the Life and Substance of Religion, as the Lean Kine, in Pharaohs Dream, did eat up the Fat. Nor lastly, Please themselves, onely in the violent Opposing of other mens Superstitions, according to the Genious of the present times; without substituting in the room of them, an inward Principle of Spirit, and Life, in their own Souls: for I fear many of us that pull down Idols in Churches, may set them up in our Hearts; and whilest we quarrel with Painted Glasse, make no scruple at all, of entertaining many foul Lusts in our Souls, and committing continuall Idolatry with them.

This in generall, was the Designe of this following Discourse, which you were pleased (Noble Senatours) not onely to expresse your good Acceptance of; but also to give a Reall Signification of your great undeserved Favour to the Authour of it. Who therefore cannot, but as the least Expression of his Thankfulnesse, humbly devote it to you; presenting it here again to your Eye, in the same Form,

in

in which it was delivered to your Eare. Desirous of nothing more, then that it might be some way usefull to You, to kindle in you, the Life and Heat of that, which is endeavoured here, to be described upon Paper: that you may expresse it, both in your private Conversations, and likewise in all your Publick Emploiments for the Common-wealth. That you may, by your kindly Influence, effectually encourage all Goodnesse: and by vertue of your Power and Authority (to use the Phrase of Solomon) scatter away all evil with your eye, *as the Sun by his Beams scattereth the Mists and Vapours.* That *from you,* Judgement may runne down like Waters, and Righteousnesse like a mighty Stream, to refresh this whole Land, that thirsteth after them. Which, whilest You distribute them plentifully to others, will bestow, both Strength and Honour to Your selves. For Justice and Righteousnesse are the Establishment of every Throne, of all Civil Power, and Authority; and if these should once forsake it, though there be Lions to support it, it could not stand long. These, together with a good Peace, well setled in a Common wealth, are all the outward Felicity we can expect, till that happy Time come, which the Prophet foretelleth, and is therefore more then a Platonicall
Idea;

Idea; *When*, the Wolf shall dwell with the Lamb, and the Leopard shall lie down with the Kid; and the Calfe, and the young Lion, and the Fatling together, and a little Child lead them: *When*, the sucking Child shall play on the hole of the Aspe, and the weaned Child shall put his hand on the Cockatrice den: *When*, they shall not hurt nor destroy in all Gods holy Mountaine; for the Earth shall be full of the knowledge of the Lord, as the waters cover the sea.

I have but one Word more, if You please to give me leave; That after your Care for the Advancement of Religion, and the Publick Good of the Common-wealth, You would think it worthy of You, to promote Ingenuous Learning, *and cast a Favourable Influence upon it. I mean not, that onely, which furnisheth the Pulpit, which you seem to be very regardfull of; but that which is more remote from such Popular use, in the severall kinds of it, which yet are all of them, both very subservient to Religion, and usefull to the Common-wealth. There is indeed a* Ψευδοπαιδεία, *as the* Philosopher *tells us, a* Bastardly kind of Literature, *and a* Ψευδώνυμος γνῶσις, *as the* Apostle *instructeth us, a* knowledge falsely so called; *which*

A

deserve

deserve not to be pleaded for. But the Noble *and* Generous Improvement *of our* Understanding Faculty, *in the true* Contemplation *of the* Wisdome, Goodnesse, *and other* Attributes *of God, in this great Fabrick of the* Universe, *cannot easily be disparaged, without a Blemish cast upon the Maker of it. Doubtlesse, we may as well enjoy, that which God hath communicated of himself to the Creatures, by this Larger faculty of our* Understandings, *as by those narrow and low faculties of our* Senses; *and yet no body counts it to be unlawfull, to hear a* Lesson *plaied upon the Lute, or to smell at a* Rose. *And these raised Improvements of our* Naturall understandings, *may be as well subservient and subordinate, to a* Divine Light *in our Minds; as the* Naturall *use of these outward Creatures here below, to the* Life of God *in our Hearts. Nay, all true* knowledge, *doth of it self naturally tend to God, who is the Fountain of it: and would ever be raising of our souls up, upon its wings thither; did not we* κατέχειν ἐν ἀδικίᾳ, *detain it, and hold it down, in* unrighteousnesse, *as the* Apostle *speaketh. All* Philosophy *to a* Wise man, *to a truly sanctified* Mind, *as he in* Plutarch *speaketh, is but* ὕλη ϛ̄ Θεολογίας, Matter for Divinity to work upon. *Religion is the*
Queen

Queen of all those inward Endowments of the Soul, and all pure Naturall knowledge, *all virgin and undeflowred* Arts & Sciences *are her Handmaids, that* rise up and call her Blessed. *I need not tell you, how much the skill of* Toungues *and* Languages, *besides the excellent use of all* Philology *in generall, conduceth to the right understanding of the Letter of Sacred* Writings, *on which the spirituall Notions must be built; for none can possibly be ignorant of that, which have but once heard of a* Translation of the Bible. *The* Apostle *exhorteth* Private Christians, to whatsoever things are lovely, whatsoever things are of good report; if there be any vertue, if there be any praise, to think on those things; *and therefore it may well become you,* (Noble Gentlemen) *in your* Publick Spheare, *to encourage so Noble a Thing as* knowledge *is, which will reflect so much* Lustre *and* Honour *back again upon your selves. That God would direct you in all your Counsels, and still blesse you and prosper you, in all your sincere Endeavours, for the* Publick Good, *is the hearty Prayer of*

    Your

          Most humble Servant,

                RALPH CUDWORTH.

I. JOHN ii. 3, 4.

And hereby we do know that we know him, if we keep his Commandments. He that saith, I know him, and keepeth not his Commandments, is a liar, and the truth is not in him.

WE have much enquiry concerning knowledge in these latter times. The sonnes of Adam are now as busie as ever himself was, about the *Tree of Knowledge* of good and evil, shaking the boughs of it, and scrambling for the fruit: whilest, I fear, many are too unmindfull of the *Tree of Life*. And though there be now no Cherubims with their flaming swords, to fright men off from it; yet the way that leads to it seems to be solitary and untrodden, as if there were but few that had any mind to tast of the Fruit of it. There be many that speak of new glimpses, and discoveries of Truth, of dawnings of Gospel-light; and no question, but God hath reserved much of this for the very Evening and Sun-set of the World, for *in the latter dayes knowledge shall be increased*: but yet I wish we could in the mean time see that *day to dawn*, which the Apostle speaks of, and that *day-starre to arise in mens hearts*. I wish whilest we talk of light, and dispute about truth, we could walk more as *children of the light*. Whereas if S. Johns rule be good here in the Text, that no man truly knows Christ, but he that keepeth his Commandments; it is much to be suspected, that many of us which pretend to light, have a thick and gloomy darknesse within over-spreading our souls. There be now many large Volumes and Discourses written concerning Christ, thousands of controversies discussed, infinite problems determined concerning his Divinity, Humanity, Union of both together; and what not? so that our bookish Christians,

that

that have all their religion in writings and papers, think they are now compleatly furnished with all kind of knowledge concerning Chrift; and when they see all their leaves lying about them, they think they have a goodly ftock of knowledge and truth, and cannot pofsibly miffe of the way to heaven; as if Religion were nothing but a little *Book-craft*, a mere *paper-skill*. But if S. Johns rule here be good, we muft not judge of our knowing of Chrift, by our skill in Books and Papers, but by our keeping of his Commandments. And that I fear will difcover many of us (notwithftanding all this light which we boaft of round about us) to have nothing but Egyptian darkneffe within upon our hearts. The vulgar fort think that they know Chrift enough, out of their Creeds and Catechifmes, and Confefsions of Faith: and if they have but a little acquainted themfelves with thefe, and like Parrets conned the words of them, they doubt not but that they are fufficiently inftructed in all the myfteries of the Kingdome of Heaven. Many of the more learned, if they can but wrangle and dispute about Christ, imagine themselves to be grown great proficients in the School of Christ. The greatest part of the world, whether learned or unlearned, think, that there is no need of purging and purifying of their hearts, for the right knowledge of Christ and his Gospel; but though their lives be never so wicked, their hearts never so foul within, yet they may know Christ sufficiently out of their Treatises and Discourses, out of their mere Systems and Bodies of Divinity; which I deny not to be usefull in a subordinate way: although our Saviour prescribeth his Disciples another method, to come to the right knowledge of Divine truths, by doing of Gods will; *he that will do my Fathers will* (saith he) *shall know of the doctrine whether it be of God.* He is a true Christian indeed, not *he* that is onely *book-taught*, but he that is *God-taught*; he that hath an *Unction from the holy one* (as our Apostle calleth it) that teacheth him all things; he that hath the Spirit of Christ within him, that *searcheth* out the *deep things of God : For as no man knoweth the things of a man, save the spirit of man*

man which is in him, even so the things of God knoweth no man but the Spirit of God. Inke and Paper can never make us Christians, can never beget a new nature, a living principle in us; can never form Christ, or any true notions of spirituall things in our hearts. The Gospel, that new Law which Christ delivered to the world, it is not merely a *Letter* without us, but a *quickning Spirit* within us. Cold Theorems and Maximes, dry and jejune Disputes, lean syllogisticall reasonings, could never yet of themselves beget the least glympse of true heavenly light, the least sap of saving knowledge in any heart. All this is but the groping of the poore dark spirit of man after truth, to find it out with his own endeavours, and feel it with his own cold and benummed hands. Words and syllables which are but dead things, cannot possibly convey the living notions of heavenly truths to us. The secret mysteries of a Divine Life, of a New Nature, of Christ formed in our hearts; they cannot be written or spoken, language and expressions cannot reach them; neither can they ever be truly understood, except the soul it self be kindled from within, and awakened into the life of them. A Painter that would draw a Rose, though he may flourish some likenesse of it in figure and colour, yet he can never paint the sent and fragrancy; or if he would draw a Flame, he cannot put a constant heat into his colours; he cannot make his pensil drop a Sound, as the Echo in the Epigramme mocks at him —— *si vis similem pingere, pinge sonum.* All the skill of cunning Artizans and Mechanicks, cannot put a principle of Life into a statue of their own making. Neither are we able to inclose in words and letters, the Life, Soul, and Essence of any Spirituall truths; & as it were to incorporate it in them. Some Philosophers have determined, that ἀρετὴ is not διδακτὸν, vertue cannot be taught by any certain rules or precepts. Men and books may propound some directions to us, that may set us in such a way of life and practice, as in which we shall at last find it within our selves, and be experimentally acquainted with it : but they cannot teach it us like a Mechanick Art or Trade. No surely, *there is a spirit in man:* and *the inspiration of the Almighty giveth this understanding.* But we

shall

shall not meet with this spirit any where, but in the way of Obedience: the knowledge of Christ, and the keeping of his Commandments, must alwayes go together, and be mutuall causes of one another.

Hereby we know that we know him, if we keep his Commandments.

He that saith, I know him, and keepeth not his Commandments, is a liar, and the truth is not in him.

I Come now unto these words themselves, which are so pregnant, that I shall not need to force out any thing at all from them: I shall therefore onely take notice of some few observations, which drop from them of their own accord, and then conclude with some Application of them to our selves.

First then, If this be the right way and methode of discovering our *knowledge of Christ*, by our *keeping of his Commandments*; Then *we may safely draw conclusions concerning our state and condition, from the conformity of our lives to the will of Christ.* Would we know whether we know Christ aright, let us consider whether the life of Christ be in us. *Qui non habet vitam Chri-*
sti

sti, Christum non habet; He that hath not the life of Christ in him, he hath nothing but the name, nothing but a phansie of Christ, he hath not the substance of him. He that builds his house upon this foundation; not an airy notion of Christ swimming in his brain, but Christ really dwelling and living in his heart; as our Saviour himself witnesseth, he *buildeth his house upon a Rock*; and when the flouds come, and the winds blow, and the rain descends, and beats upon it, it shall stand impregnably. But he that builds all his comfort upon an ungrounded perswasion, that God from all eternity hath loved him, and absolutely decreed him to life and happinesse, and seeketh not for God really dwelling in his soul; he builds his house upon a Quicksand, and it shall suddenly sink and be swallowed up: *his hope shall be cut off, & his trust shall be a spiders web; he shall lean upon his house, but it shall not stand, he shall hold it fast but it shall not endure.* We are no where commanded to pry into these secrets, but the wholesome counsell and advise given us, is this; to *make our calling and election sure.* We have no warrant in Scripture, to peep into these hidden
Rolls

Rolls and Volumes of Eternity, and to make it our firſt thing that we do when we come to Chriſt, to ſpell out our names in the ſtarres, and to perſwade our ſelves that we are certainly elected to everlaſting happineſſe: before we ſee the *image of God*, in righteouſneſſe and true holineſſe, ſhaped in our hearts. Gods everlaſting decree, is too dazeling and bright an object for us at firſt to ſet our eye upon: it is far eaſier and ſafer for us to look upon the raies of his goodneſſe and holineſſe as they are reflected in our own hearts; and there to read the mild and gentle Characters of Gods love to us, in our love to him, and our hearty compliance with his heavenly will: as it is ſafer for us if we would ſee the Sunne, to look upon it here below in a pale of water; then to caſt up our daring eyes upon the body of the Sun it ſelf, which is too radiant and ſcorching for us. The beſt aſſurance that any one can have of his intereſt in God, is doubtleſſe the conformity of his ſoul to him. Thoſe divine purpoſes, whatſoever they be are altogether unſearchable and unknowable by us, they lie wrapt up in everlaſting darkneſſe, and covered in a deep Abysse; who is able to fathom the bottome of them? Let us not therefore make this our first attempt towards God and Religion, to perswade our selves strongly of these everlasting Decrees: for if at our first flight we aime so high, we shall happily but scorch our wings, and be struck back with lightning, as those *Giants* of old were, that would needs attempt to invade and assault heaven. And it is indeed a most *Giganticall* Essay, to thrust our selves so boldly into the lap of heaven; it is the pranck of a *Nimrod*, of a *mighty Hunter* thus rudely to deal with God, and to force heaven and happinesse before his face whether he will or no. The way to obtain a good assurance indeed of our title to heaven, is not to clamber up to it, by a ladder of our own ungrounded perswasions; but to dig as low as hell by humility and self-denyall in our own hearts: and though this may seem to be the furthest way about; yet it is indeed the neerest, and safest way to it. We must ἀναβαίνειν κάτω and καταβαίνειν ἄνω, as the Greek Epigramme speaks, *ascend downward, & descend upward*; if we would indeed come to heaven,

ven, or get any true perswasion of our title to it. The most gallant and triumphant confidence of a Christian, riseth safely and surely upon this low foundation, that lies deep under ground; and there stands firmly and stedfastly. When our heart is once tuned into a conformity with the word of God, when we feel our will, perfectly to concurre with his will, we shal then presently perceive a *Spirit of adoption* within our selves, teaching us to cry *Abba. Father*. We shall not then care for peeping into those hidden Records of Eternity, to see whether our names be written there in golden characters: no, we shall find a copy of Gods thoughts concerning us, written in our own breasts. There we may read the characters of his favour to us, there we may feel an inward sense of his love to us, flowing out of our hearty and unfained love to him. And we shall be more undoubtedly perswaded of it, then if any of those winged *Watchmen* above, that are privie to heavens secrets, should come & tel us; that they saw our names enrolled in those *volumes of eternity*. Whereas on the contrary; though we strive to perswade our selves never so confidently, that God from all eternity hath loved us, and elected us to life and happinesse; if we do yet in the mean time entertain any iniquity within our hearts, and willingly close with any lust; do what we can, we shall find many a cold qualme ever now and then seizing upon us at approching dangers; and when death it self shall grimly look us in the face, we shall feel our hearts even to die within us, and our spirits quite faint away, though we strive to raise them and recover them never so much, with the *Strong Waters* and *Aqua vitæ* of our own ungrounded presumptions. The least inward lust willingly continued in, will be like a *worme*, fretting the *Gourd* of our jolly confidence, and presumptuous perswasion of Gods love, and alwayes gnawing at the root of it: and though we strive to keep it alive, and continually besprinkle it with some dews of our own; yet it will alwayes be dying and withering in our bosomes. But a good Conscience within, will be alwayes better to a Christian, then *health to his navell, and marrow to his bones*; it will be an everlasting cordiall to his heart: it will be softer to him then

then a bed of doune, and he may sleep securely upon it, in the midst of raging and tempestuous seas; when the winds bluster, and the waves beat round about him. A good conscience, is the best looking-glasse of heaven; in which the soul may see God's thoughts and purposes concerning it, as so many shining starres reflected to it. *Hereby we know that we know Christ, hereby we know that Christ loves us, if we keep his Commandments.*

Secondly, If hereby onely we know that we know Christ, by our keeping his Commandments; *Then the knowledge of Christ doth not consist merely in a few barren Notions, in a form of certain dry and saplesse Opinions.* Christ came not into the world to fil our heads with mere Speculations; to kindle a fire of wrangling and contentious dispute amongst us, and to warm our spirits against one another with nothing but angry & peevish debates, whilst in the mean time our hearts remain all ice within towards God, aud have not the least spark of true heavenly fire to melt and thaw them. Christ came not to possesse our brains onely with some cold opinions, that

send

send down nothing but a freezing and benumming influence upon our hearts. Christ was *Vitæ Magister*, not *Scholæ*: and he is the best Christian, whose heart beats with the truest pulse towards heaven; not he whose head spinneth out the finest cobwebs. He that endeavours really to mortifie his lusts, and to comply with that truth in his life, which his Conscience is convinced of; is neerer a Christian, though he never heard of Christ; then he that believes all the vulgar Articles of the Christian faith, and plainly denyeth Christ in his life. Surely, the way to heaven that Christ hath taught us, is plain and easie, if we have but honest hearts: we need not many Criticismes, many School-distinctions, to come to a right understanding of it. Surely, Christ came not to ensnare us and intangle us with captious niceties, or to pusle our heads with deep speculations, and lead us through hard and craggie notions into the Kingdome of heaven. I perswade my self, that no man shall ever be kept out of heaven, for not comprehending mysteries that were beyond the reach of his shallow understanding; if he had but an honest and

and good heart, that was ready to comply with Chrifts Commandments. *Say not in thine heart,* **Who** *fhall afcend into heaven?* that is, with high fpeculations to bring down Chrift from thence: or, *Who fhall defcend into the abyffe beneath?* that is with deep fearching thoughts to fetch up Chrift from thence: but loe, *the word is nigh thee, even in thy mouth, and in thy heart.* But I wifh, it were not the diftemper of our times, to fcare and fright men onely with *opinions,* and make them onely folicitous about the entertaining of this and that fpeculation, which will not render them any thing the better in their lives, or the liker unto God; whilft in the mean time there is no fuch care taken about *keeping of Chrifts* Commandments, and being renewed in our minds according to the image of God, in righteoufneffe and true holineffe. We fay, *Loe, here is Chrift;* and *Loe, there is Chrift,* in thefe and thefe *opinions;* whereas in truth, Chrift is neither here, nor there, nor any where; but where the Spirit of Chrift, where the life of Chrift is. Do we not now adayes open and lock up heaven, with the private key of this and that opinion,

on of our own according to our severall fancies as we please? And if any one observe Chrifts Commandments never so sincerely, and serve God, with faith and a pure conscience, that yet happely skils not of some contended for *opinions*, some darling *notions*; he hath not the right Shibboleth, he hath not the true Watch-word; he must not passe the Guards into heaven. Do we not make this and that *opinion*, this and that outward *form*, to be the *Wedding-garment*, and boldly sentence those to outer darknesse, that are not invested therewith? Whereas every true Christian, finds the least dram of hearty affection towards God, to be more cordiall and soveriegn to his soul; then all the *speculative notions*, and *opinions* in the world: and though he study also to inform his understanding aright, and free his mind from all errour and misapprehensions; yet it is nothing but the *life of Christ* deeply rooted in his heart which is the Chymicall Elixer that he feeds upon. Had he *all faith that he could remove mountains* (as S. Paul speaks) had he *all knowledge, all tongues and languages*; yet he prizeth one dram of love beyond them all. He
ac-

accounteth him that feeds upon mere *notions* in Religion, to be but an aiery and Chamelion like Christian. He findeth himself now otherwise rooted and centred in God, then when he did before merely contemplate and gaze upon him: he tasteth and relisheth God within himself, he hath *quendam saporem Dei, a certain savour of him;* whereas before he did but rove and guesse at random at him. He feeleth himself safely anchored in God, and will not be disswaded from it; though perhaps he skill not many of those *subtleties*, which others make the Alpha and Omega of their Religion. Neither is he scared with those childish affrightments, with which some would force their private conceits upon him; he is above the superstitious dreading, of mere speculative opinions; as well as the superstitious reverence of outward ceremonies: he cares not so much for subtlety, as for soundnesse and health of mind. And indeed, as it was well spoken by a noble Philosopher, ἄνευ ἀρετῆς Θεὸς ὄνομα μόνον, that *without purity and virtue God is nothing but an empty name;* so it is as true here, that without obedience to Christs

Commandments, without the *life of Christ* dwelling in us, whatsoever *opinions* we entertain of him, Christ is but onely named by us, he is not *known*. I speak not here against a free and ingenuous enquiry into all Truth, according to our severall abilities and opportunities, I plead not for the captivating and enthralling of our judgements to the Dictates of men, I do not disparage the naturall improvement of our understanding faculties by true Knowledge, which is so noble and gallant a perfection of the mind: but the thing which I aime against is, the dispiriting of the life and vigour of our Religion, by dry speculations, and making it nothing but a mere dead skeleton of *opinions*, a few dry bones without any flesh and sinews tyed up together: and the misplacing of all our zeal upon an eager prosecution of these, which should be spent to better purpose upon other objects. Knowledge indeed is a thing farre more excellent then riches, outward pleasures, worldly dignities, or any thing else in the world besides Holinesse, and the Conformity of our wills to the will of God: but yet our happinesse consisteth not

in

in it, but in a certain Divine Temper & Constitution of soul which is farre above it. But it is a piece of that corruption that runneth through humane nature, that we naturally prize Truth, more then Goodnesse; Knowledge, more then Holinesse. We think it a gallant thing to be fluttering up to Heaven with our wings of Knowledge and Speculation: whereas the highest mystery of a Divine Life here, and of perfect Happinesse hereafter, consisteth in nothing but mere Obedience to the Divine Will. Happinesse is nothing but that inward sweet delight, that will arise from the Harmonious agreement between our wills and Gods will. There is nothing contrary to God in the whole world, nothing that fights against him but *Self will*. This is the strong Castle, that we all keep garrison'd against heaven in every one of our hearts, which God continually layeth siege unto: and it must be conquered and demolished, before we can conquer heaven. It was by reason of this *Self-will*, that Adam fell in Paradise; that those glorious Angels, those *Morning-starres*, kept not their first station, but dropt down from heaven like Falling Starres, and sunk into this condition of bitternesse, anxiety, and wretchednesse in which now they are. They all intangled themselves with the length of their own wings, they would needs will more and otherwise then God would will in them: and going about to make their wills wider, and to enlarge them into greater amplitude; the more they strugled, they found themselves the faster pinioned, & crowded up into narrownesse and servility; insomuch that now they are not able to use any wings at all, but inheriting the *serpents* curse, can onely creep with their *bellies* upon the earth. Now our onely way to recover God & happines again, is not to soar up with our Understandings, but to destroy this *Self-will* of ours: and then we shall find our wings to grow again, our plumes fairly spread, & our selves raised aloft into the free Aire of perfect Liberty, which is perfect Happinesse. There is nothing in the whole world able to do us good or hurt, but *God* and our own *Will*; neither riches nor poverty, nor disgrace nor honour, nor life nor death, nor Angels nor Divels; but Willing or Not-willing as we ought to do.

do. Should Hell it self cast all its fiery darts against us, if our *Will* be right, if it be informed by the Divine Will; they can do us no hurt; we have then, (if I may so speak,) an inchanted Shield that is impenetrable, and will beare off all. God will not hurt us, and Hell cannot hurt us, if we will nothing but what God wills. Nay, then we are acted by God himself, and the whole Divinity floweth in upon us; and when we have cashiered this *Self-will* of ours, which did but shackle and confine our soules, our wills shall then become truly free, being widened and enlarged to the extent of Gods own will. *Hereby we know that we know Christ indeed,* not by our *Speculative Opinions* concerning him, *but by our keeping of his Commandments.*

Thirdly, if hereby we are to judge whether we truly *know Christ,* by our *keeping of his Commandments;* so that *he that saith he knoweth him, and keepeth not his Commandments, is a lyar;* Then, *This was not the Plot and designe of the Gospel, to give the world an indulgence to sin, upon what pretence soever.* Though we are too prone, to make such misconstructions of it: as if God had

had intended nothing elſe in it, but to *dandle* our corrupt nature, and contrive a ſmooth and eaſie way for us to come to happineſſe, without the toilſome labour of ſubduing our luſts and ſinfull affections. Or, As if the Goſpel were nothing elſe but a Declaration to the World, of Gods ingaging his affections from all eternity, on ſome particular perſons, in ſuch a manner, as that he would reſolve to love them, and dearly embrace them, though he never made them partakers of his Image in righteouſneſſe and true holineſſe: and though they ſhould remain under the power of all their luſts, yet they ſhould ſtill continue his *beloved ones*, and he would notwithſtanding, at laſt bring them undoubtedly into heaven. Which is nothing elſe, but to make the God that we worſhip, the God of the new Teſtament, a προσωπολήπτης, *an accepter of perſons* : and one that ſhould encourage that in the world which is diametrally oppoſite to Gods own Life and Being. And indeed nothing is more ordinary, then for us to ſhape out ſuch monſtrous and deformed Notions of God unto our ſelves, by looking upon him through the *coloured Medium* of our own

own corrupt hearts, and having the *eye* of our soul *tinctured* by the suffusions of our own lusts. And therefore, because we mortalls can *fondly* love and hate, and sometimes, hug the very Vices, of those to whom our affections are engaged, and kisse their very Deformities; we are so ready to shape out a Deity like unto our selves, and to fashion out such a *God*, as will in Christ at least, hug the very wickednesse of the world: and in those that be once his own, by I know not what, *fond* affection, appropriated to himself, connive at their very sinnes, so that they shall not make the least breach betwixt himself and them. Truly, I know not whether of the two, be the worse Idolatry, and of the deeper stain; for a man to make a god out of *a piece of wood*, and *fall down unto it and worship it, and say, Deliver me, for thou art my God*, as it is expressed in the Prophet *Isaiah*; or to set up such an Idol-god of our own Imagination as this is, fashioned out according to the similitude of our own *fondnesse* and wickednesse: and when we should paint out God with the liveliest Colours, that we can possibly borrow from any created being, with

with the purest Perfections that we can abstract from them; to draw him out thus with the blackest Coal of our own corrupt hearts; and to make the very blots and blurs of our own souls, to be the Letters, which we spell out his name by. Thus do we that are Children of the Night, make black and ugly representations of God unto our selves, as the *Ethiopians* were wont to do, copying him out according to our own likenesse; and setting up that unto our selves for a God, which we love most dearly in our selves, that is, our Lusts. But there is no such *God* as this any where in the world, but onely in some mens false imaginations, who know not all this while, that they look upon themselves instead of God, and make an Idol of themselves, which they worship and adore for him; being so full of themselves, that whatsoever they see round about them, even God himself, they colour with their own Tincture: like him that *Aristotle* speaks of, that wheresoever he went, and whatsoever he looked upon, he saw still his own face, as in a glasse, represented to him. And therefore it is no wonder if men seem naturally

more

more devoutly affected tovvard such an Imaginary God, as we have now described, then to the True Reall God, clothed with his own proper Attributes; since it is nothing but an Image of themselves, which *Narcissuslike* they fall in love with: no wonder if they kisse and dandle such a *Baby-god* as this, which like little children, they have dressed up out of the clouts of their own fond Phancies, according to their own liknesse, of purpose that they might play and sport with it. But God will ever *dwell* in spotlesse *light*, howsoever we paint him and disfigure him here below: he will still be circled about, with his own raies of unstained and immaculate glory. And though the Gospel be not God, as he is in his own *Brightnesse*, but God *Vailed* and *Masked* to us, God in a state of Humiliation, and Condescent, as the Sun in a Rainbow; yet it is nothing else but a clear and unspotted Mirrour of Divine Holinesse, Goodnesse, Purity; in which Attributes lies the very Life and Essence of God himself. The Gospel is nothing else, but God descending into the World in *Our Form*, and conversing with us in our likenesse; that he might

might allure, and draw us up to God, and make us partakers of his *Divine Form*. Θεὸς γέγονεν ἄνθρωπος (as *Athanasius* speaks) ἵνα ἡμᾶς ἐν ἑαυτῷ θεαποιήσῃ, *God was therefore incarnated and made man, that he might Deifie us*, that is, (as S. *Peter* expresseth it) make us *partakers of the Divine nature*. Now, I say, the very proper Character, and Essentiall Tincture of God himself, is nothing else but *Goodnesse*. Nay, I may be bold to adde, That God is therefore God, because he is the highest and most perfect Good: and Good is not therefore Good, because God out of an arbitrary will of his, would have it so. Whatsoever God doth in the World, he doth it as it is suitable to the highest Goodnesse; the first Idea, and fairest Copy of which is his own Essence. Vertue and Holinesse in creatures, as *Plato* well discourseth in his *Euthyphro*, are not *therefore Good, because God loveth them*, and will have them be accounted such; but rather, *God therefore loveth them because they are in themselves simply good.* Some of our own Authors, go a little further yet, and tell us; that God doth not fondly love himself, because he is *himself*, but therefore he loveth him-

himself because he is the highest and most absolute *Goodnesse*: so that if there could be any thing in the world better then God, God would love that better then himself: but because he is Essentially the most perfect *Good*; therefore he cannot but love his own *goodnesse*, infinitely above all other things. And it is another mistake which sometimes we have of God, by shaping him out according to the Model of our selves, when we make him nothing but a *blind, dark, impetuous Self will*, running through the world; such as we our selves are furiously acted with, that have not the Ballast of *absolute goodnesse* to poize and settle us. That I may therefore come nearer to the thing in hand: God who is *absolute goodnesse*, cannot love any of his Creatures & take pleasure in them, without bestowing a communication of his Goodnesse and Likenesse upon them. God cannot make a Gospel, to promise men Life & Happinesse hereafter, without being *regenerated*, & made partakers of his *holinesse*. As soon may Heaven and Hell, be reconciled together, and lovingly shake hands with one another; as God can be fondly indulgent to any sinne, in whomsoever it be. As soon may Light and Darknesse be espoused together, and Mid-night be married to the Noon-day; as God can be joyned in a league of friendship, to any wicked Soul.

The great Designe of God in the Gospel, is to clear up this Mist of Sin and Corruption, which we are here surrounded vvith: and to bring up his creatures, out of the *shadow of death*, to the *Region of Light* above, the Land of Truth and Holinesse. The great Mystery of the Gospel, is to establish a *Godlike* frame and disposition of spirit, which consists in Righteousnesse and true Holinesse, in the hearts of men. And Christ, who is the great and mighty Saviour, he came on purpose into the World; not onely to save us from *Fire and Brimstone*, but also to save us from our *Sins*. Christ hath therefore made an Expiation of our sins, by his death upon the Crosse, that we being thus *delivered out of the hands of* these our greatest *enemies, might serve God without fear, in holinesse and righteousnesse before him, all the dayes of our life.* This *grace of God that bringeth salvation*, hath therefore *appeared to all men*, in the Gospel, that it might

teach

teach us to deny ungodlinesse and worldly lusts, and that we should live soberly, righteously, and godlily in this present world: looking for that blessed hope, and glorious appearing of the great God, and our Saviour Jesus Christ; who gave himself for us, that he might redeem us from all iniquity, and purifie unto himself a peculiar people, Zealous of good works. These things I write unto you (saith our *Apostle* a little before my text) *that you sinne not:* therein expressing the end of the whole Gospel, which is, not onely to *cover sinne*, by spreading the Purple Robe of Chrifts death and sufferings over it, whilst it still remaineth in us with all its filth and noisomnesse unremoved; but also, to convey a powerfull and mighty Spirit of holinesse, to *cleanse* us, and *free* us from it. And this is a greater grace of Gods to us, then the former, which still go both together in the Gospel; besides the free remission and pardon of sinne in the *bloud of Christ*, the delivering of us from the power of sinne, by the *Spirit of Christ* dwelling in our hearts. Christ came not into the world onely, to cast a Mantle over us, and hide all our filthy sores, from Gods avenging eye, with his merits and righteousnesse;

but

but he came likewise, to be a Chirurgeon, and Physitian of souls, to free us from the filth and corruption of them; which is more grievous and burdensome, more noysome to a true Christian, then the guilt of sinne it self. Should a poore wretched, and diseased creature, that is full of sores and ulcers, be covered all over with Purple, or clothed with Scarlet; he would take but little contentment in it, whilest his sores, and wounds, remain upon him: and he had much rather be arraied in rags, so he might obtain but soundnesse and health within. The Gospel is a true *Bethesda, a pool of Grace*, where such poore, lame, and infirme creatures, as we are, upon the moving of Gods spirit in it, may descend down, not onely to wash our skin and outside, but also to be cured of our diseases within. And what ever the world thinks, there is a powerfull Spirit that *moves upon these waters*, the waters of the Gospel, for this new Creation, the Regeneration of souls; the very same Spirit, that once *moved* upon *the waters* of the universe at the first Creation, and spreading its mighty wings over them, did hatch the new born World

into

into this perfection: I say, the same *Almighty spirit* of Christ, still worketh in the Gospel, spreading its gentle, healing, quickening wings, over our souls. The Gospel, is not like *Abana* and *Pharphar*, those common Rivers of *Damascus*, that could onely cleanse the outside; but it is a true *Jordan*, in which such leprouse *Naamans*, as we all are, may *Wash* and be clean. *Blessed indeed are they, whose iniquities are forgiven, and whose sinnes are covered: Blessed is the man to whom the Lord will not impute sinne*: but yet, rather Blessed are they, whose sinnes are removed like a *Morning-cloud*, and quite taken away from them: *Blessed*, thrice blessed, *are they, that hunger and thirst after righteousnesse, for they shall be satisfied: Blessed are the pure in heart for they shall see God.* Our Saviour Christ came (as *John* the *Baptist* tells us) *with a Fan in his hand, that he might throughly purge his floore and gather his wheat into his garner: but the chaff he will burn up, with unquenchable fire.* He came (as the Prophet *Malachy* speaks) *like a Refiners fire, and like Fullers sope; to sit as a Refiner and Purifier of silver, and to purifie all the sonnes of Levi, and purge them as gold and silver, that they*

may

may offer unto the Lord an offering in righteousnesse. Christ came not onely, to write *Holinesse to the Lord* upon *Aarons* forehead, and to put his *Urim* and *Thummim* upon his Breast-plate, but *This is the Covenant, saith the Lord, that I will make with them in those dayes; I will put my Law into their inward parts, and write it in their hearts, and then I will be their God, and they shall be my people: they shall be all Kings and Priests unto me. God sent his own sonne* (saith S^t. *Paul*) *in the likenesse of sinfull flesh, and by a sacrifice for sinne, condemned sinne in the flesh: that the righteousnesse of the Law might be fulfilled in us, who walk not after the flesh, but after the Spirit.* The *first Adam*, as the Scripture tells us, brought in a reall defilement, which like a noisome Leprosie, hath overspread all mankind: and therefore *the second Adam* must not onely fill the World with a *conceit*, of Holinesse, and meer Imaginary Righteousnesse; but he must really convey, such an *immortall seed* of Grace into the hearts of true Believers, as may prevaile still more and more in them, till it have at last, quite wrought out that *poison* of the *Serpent.* Christ, that was nothing, but *Divinity dwelling in a Tabernacle of*
flesh,

flesh, and God himself immediatly acting a humane nature; he came into the World to kindle here that *Divine life* amongst men, which is certainly dearer unto God, then any thing else whatsoever in the World; and to propagate this Celestiall fire, from one heart still unto another, untill the end of the World. Neither is he, or was he ever absent from this Spark of his Divinity, kindled amongst men, wheresoever it be, though he seem bodily to be withdrawn from us. He is the standing, constant, inexhausted Fountain, of this divine Light and Heat; that still toucheth every soul that is enlivened by it, with an out-stretched Ray, and freely lends his Beams, and disperseth his *influence* to all, from the beginning of the World to the end of it. *We all receive of his fulnesse, grace for grace,* as all the Starres in heaven, are said to light their Candles at the Suns flame. For though his body be withdrawn from us, yet by the lively and *virtuall Contact* of his Spirit, he is always kindling, cheering, quickening, warming, enlivening hearts. Nay, this *Divine life* begun and kindled in any heart, wheresoever it be, is *something of God in flesh*;

and

and, in a sober and qualified sence, *Divinity incarnate*; and all particular Christians, that are really possessed of it, so many *Mysticall Christs*. And God forbid, that *Gods own Life* and *Nature* here in the World, should be forlorn, forsaken, and abandoned of God himself. Certainly, where-ever it is, though never so little, like a sweet, young, tender *Babe*, once born in any heart; when it crieth unto God the *father* of it, with pitifull and bemoning looks imploring his compassion; it cannot chuse but move his *fatherly bowels*, and make them *yerne*, and turn towards it, and by strong sympathy, draw his compassionate arm to help and relieve it. Never was any tender Infant, so dear to those Bowels that begat it as an *Infant new-born Christ, formed in the heart* of any true believer, to God the *father* of it. Shall the *children of this World*, the *sonnes of darknesse*, be moved with such tender affection, and compassion, towards the fruit of their bodies, their own Naturall offspring; and shall God who is the *Father of lights*, the fountain of all goodnesse, be moved with no compassion towards his true Spirituall Offspring, and have no regard
to

to those sweet *Babes of Light*, ingendered by his own beams in mens hearts, that in their lovely countenances, bear the resemblance of his own face, and call him their *father*? Shall he see them lie fainting, and gasping, and dying here in the World, for want of nothing to preserve and keep them, but an *Influence* from him, who first gave them life and breath? No; hear the language of Gods heart, heare *the sounding of his bowels* towards them: *Is it Ephraim my dear sonne? Is it that pleasant child? since I spake of him I do earnestly remember him, my bowels, my bowels are troubled for him; I will surely have mercy upon him, saith the Lord*. If those expressions of goodnesse and tender affection here amongst creatures, be but drops of that full Ocean that is in God; how can we then imagine, that this *Father* of our *spirits*, should have so little regard to his own dear Offspring, I do not say our souls, but that which is the very Life and Soul of our souls, the *Life of God* in us; which is nothing else but Gods own Self communicated to us, his own Sonne born in our hearts; as that he should suffer it to be cruelly murdered in its *Infancy* by our Sinnes, and like young *Hercules* in its very *cradle*, to be strangled by those filthy *vipers*; that he should see him to be crucified by wicked *Lusts*, nailed fast to the crosse by invincible *Corruptions*; pierced and gored on every side with the poisoned spears of the Devils *temptations*, and at last to give up the Ghost; and yet his tender heart not at all relent, nor be all this while impassionated with so sad a spectacle? Surely, we cannot think he hath such an *adamantine* breast, such a *flinty* nature as this is. What then? must we say that though indeed he be willing, yet he is not able, to rescue his crucified and tormented *Sonne*, now bleeding upon the crosse; to *take him down* from thence *and save him*? Then must Sinne be more powerfull then God: that weak, crasie, and sickly thing, more strong then the *Rock of ages*: and the Devil the Prince of Darknesse, more mighty, then the God of Light. No surely, there is a weaknesse and impotency in all Evil, a masculine strength and vigour in all Goodnesse: and therefore doubtlesse the *Highest Good*, the πρῶτον ἀγαθὸν as the Philosophers call it, is the strongest thing in the World.

Nil

Nil potentius Summo Bono. Gods Power displaied in the World, is nothing but his *Goodnesse* strongly reaching all things, from heighth to depth, from the highest Heaven, to the lowest Hell: and irresistibly imparting it self to every thing, according to those severall degrees in which it is capable of it. Have the Fiends of Darknesse then, those poore forlorn spirits, that are fettered and locked up in the Chaines of their own wickednesse, any strength to withstand the force of infinite *Goodnesse*, which is infinite Power? or do they not rather skulk in holes of darknesse, and flie like Bats and Owls, before the approching beams of this Sun of Righteousnesse? Is God powerfull to kill and to destroy, to damne and to torment, and is he not powerfull to save? Nay, it is the sweetest Flower in all the Garland of his Attributes, it is the richest Diamond in his Crown of Glory, that he is *Mighty to save*: and this is farre more magnificent for him, then to be stiled *Mighty to destroy*. For that, except it be in the way of Justice, speaks no Power at all, but mere Impotency, for the Root of all Power, is Goodnesse. Or must we say lastly, that God indeed

indeed is able to rescue us out of the Power of sinne & Satan, when we sigh & grone towards him, but yet sometimes to exercise his absolute Authority, his uncontrollable Dominion, he delights rather in plunging wretched souls down into infernall Night, & everlasting Darknesse? What shall we then make the God of the whole World? Nothing but a cruell and dreadfull *Erynnis*, with *curled fiery Snakes* about his head, and *Firebrands* in his hands, thus governing the World? Surely this will make us either secretly to think, that there is no God at all in the World, if he must needs be such, or else to wish heartily, there were none. But doubtlesse, God will at last, confute all these our *Misapprehensions* of him, he will unmask our *Hypocriticall pretences*, and clearly cast the shame of all our sinfull Deficiencies, upon our selves, and vindicate his own Glory from receiving the least stain or blemish by them. In the mean time, let us know, that the Gospel now requireth, far more of us, then ever the Law did; for it requireth a *New Creature*, a *Divine Nature*, *Christ formed in us*: but yet withall, it bestoweth a *quickening Spirit*, an
enlivening

enlivening Power to inable us, to expresse that, which is required of us. Whosoever therefore truly *knows Christ, the same also keepeth Christs Commandments. But, he that saith, I know him, and keepeth not his Commandments, he is a liar, and the truth is not in him.*

I Have now done with the *First part* of my Discourse, concerning those *Observations,* which arise naturally from the Words, and offer themselves to us: I shall in the next place, proceed to make some generall *Application* of them, all together.

NOw therefore, I beseech you, Let us consider, whether or no we know *Christ* indeed: Not by our acquaintance with *Systems and Modells* of Divinity; not by our skill in *Books* and *Papers*; but by our *keeping of Christs Commandments*. All the Books and writings which we converse with, they can but represent spirituall Objects to our understandings; which yet we can never see in their own true Figure, Colour, and Proportion, untill we have a *Divine light* within, to

irrradiate

irradiate, and shine upon them. Though there be never such excellent truths concerning Christ, and his Gospel, set down in words and letters; yet they will be but unknown Characters to us, untill we have a *Living spirit* within us, that can decypher them: untill the same Spirit, by secret Whispers in our hearts, do comment upon them, which did at first endite them. There be many that understand, the Greek and Hebrew of the *Scripture*, the Originall Languages in which the Text was written, that never understood the *Language of the spirit*. There is a *Caro* and a *Spiritus*, a *Flesh* and a *Spirit*, a *Bodie* and a *Soul*, in all the writings of the Scriptures: it is but the *Flesh*, and *Body*, of Divine Truths, that is printed upon Paper; which many Moths of Books and Libraries, do onely feed upon; many Walking Scheletons of knowledge, that bury and entombe Truths, in the Living Sepulchres of their souls, do onely converse with: such as never did any thing else, but pick at the mere Bark and Rind of Truths, and crack the Shels of them. But there is a *Soul*, and *Spirit* of divine Truths, that could never yet be congealed into Inke,

Inke, that could never be blotted upon Paper, which by a secret traduction and conveiance, passeth from one Soul unto another; being able to dwell and lodge no where, but in a Spirituall being, in a Living thing; because it self is nothing but *Life* and *Spirit*. Neither can it, where indeed it is, expresse it self sufficiently in Words and Sounds, but it will best declare and speak it self in Actions: as the old manner of *writing* among the Egyptians was, not by Words, but Things. The *Life* of divine Truths, is better expressed in Actions then in Words, because Actions are more *Living* things, then words; Words, are nothing but the dead Resemblances, and Pictures of those Truths, which *live* and *breath* in Actions: and the *Kingdome of* God (as the Apostle speaketh) *consisteth not in Word*, but in Life, and *Power*. Τὰ πρόβατα, ὁ χόρτον φέροντα τοῖς ποιμέσιν ἐπιδεικνύει πόσον ἔφαγεν· (saith the Morall Philosopher) ἀλλὰ τὴν νομὴν ἔσω πέψαντα, ἔριον ἔξω φέρει ἃ γάλα· *Sheep do not come, and bring their Fodder to their Shepheard, and shew him how much they eat, but inwardly concocting and digesting it, they make it appear, by the Fleece which they wear upon their*

their backs, and by the Milke which they give. And let not us Christians affect onely to talk and dispute of Christ, and so measure our knowledge of him by our words; but let us shew ἀπὸ τῶν θεωρημάτων περφγέντων τὰ ἔργα, our *knowledge concocted* into our lives and actions; and then let us really manifest that we are Christs *Sheep* indeed, that we are his *Disciples,* by that *Fleece* of Holinesse, which we wear, and by the *Fruits* that we dayly yield in our lives and conversations: for *herein* (saith Christ) *is my Father glorified, that ye bear much fruit; so shall ye be my Disciples.* Let us not (I beseech you) judge of our *knowing Christ,* by our ungrounded *Perswasions* that Christ from all Eternity hath loved us, and given himself particularly for Us, without the Conformity of our lives to *Christs Commandments,* without the reall partaking of the Image of Christ in our hearts. The great Mysterie of the Gospel, it doth not lie onely in *Christ without us,* (though we must know also what he hath done for us) but the very Pith and Kernel of it, consists in *Christ inwardly formed* in our hearts. Nothing is truly Ours, but what lives in our Spirits.

Spirits. *Salvation* it self cannot *save* us, as long as it is onely without us; no more then *Health* can cure us, and make us sound, when it is not within us, but somewhere at distance from us; no more then *Arts and Sciences*, whilst they lie onely in Books and Papers without us, can make us learned. The Gospel, though it be a Sovereigne and Medicinall thing in it self, yet the mere knowing and believing of the history of it, will do us no good: we can receive no vertue from it, till it be inwardly digested & concocted into our souls; till it be made *Ours*, and become a *living thing* in our hearts. The Gospel, if it be onely without us, cannot save us; no more then that Physitians Bill, could cure the ignorant Patient of his disease, who, when it was commended to him, took the Paper onely, and put it up in his pocket, but never drunk the Potion that was prescribed in it. All that Christ did for us in the flesh, when he was here upon earth; From his lying in a *Manger*, when he was born in *Bethlehem*, to his bleeding upon the *Crosse* on *Golgotha*; it will not save us from our sinnes, unlesse Christ by his Spirit dwell in us. It will not avail us, to believe that he was born of a *Virgin*, unlesse the *power of the most High overshadow* our hearts, and beget him there likewise. It will not profit us, to believe that he died upon the *Crosse* for us; unlesse we be *baptized into his death*, by the Mortification of all our lusts; unlesse *the old man of sinne be crucified* in our hearts. Christ indeed hath made an Expiation for our sinnes upon his Crosse; and the Bloud of Christ is the onely sovereign Balsame to free us from the guilt of them: but yet besides the *sprinkling* of the *bloud* of Christ upon us, we must be made partakers also of his *spirit*. Christ came into the World, as well to redeem us from the power and bondage of our sinnes, as to free us from the guilt of them. *You know* (saith S. *John*) *that he was manifested, to take away our sinnes; whosoever therefore abideth in him, sinneth not, whosoever sinneth, hath not seen nor known him.* Loe the end of Christs coming into the World, Loe a designe worthy of *God manifested in the flesh*. Christ did not take all those paines; to lay aside his Robes of Glory, and come down hither into the World; to enter into a Virgins wombe; to be born in our humane shape,

shape, and be laid a poore crying infant in a Manger; & having no *form nor comlinesse* at all upon him, to take upon him the *Form of a servant*; to undergo a reprochfull and ignominious life, and at last to be abandoned to a shamefull death, a death upon the Crosse; I say, he did not do all this, merely to bring in a *Notion* into the World, without producing any reall and substantiall effect at all, without the changing, mending, and reforming of the World: so that men should still be as wicked as they were before, and as much under the power of the Prince of Darknesse; onely, they should not be *thought so*: they should still remain as full of all the filthy sores, of sinne & corruption as before; onely, they should be *accounted whole*. Shall God come down from heaven, & *pitch* a *Tabernacle* amongst men? Shall he undertake such a huge Designe, and make so great a noise of doing something, which, when it is all summed up, shall not at last amount to a *Reality*? Surely, Christ did not undergo all this to so little purpose; he would not take all this paines for us, that he might be able at last, to put into our hands, nothing but a Blanck. He

was

was with child, he was in pain and travel, and hath *he brought forth nothing but wind,* hath he been delivered *of the Eastwind*? Is that great designe that was so long carried in the Wombe of Eternity, now proved abortive, or else nothing but a mere windy birth? No surely, The end of the Gospel is *Life* and *Perfection,* 'tis a *Divine nature,* 'tis a *Godlike* frame and disposition of spirit, 'tis to make us partakers of the *Image of God* in Righteousnesse and true Holinesse, without which, Salvation it self were but a Notion. Christ came indeed into the World, to make an Expiation and Atonement for our sinnes, but the end of this was, that we might eschew sinne, that we might forsake *all ungodlinesse and worldly lusts.* The Gospel declares pardon of sinne to those, that are *heavy laden* with it, and willing to be disburdened, to this end, that it might quicken and enliven us to new obedience. Whereas otherwise, the *Guilt* of sinne might have detained us in horrour and despair, and so have kept us still more strongly under the *Power* of it, in sad and dismall apprehensions of Gods wrath provoked against us, and inevitably falling on us. But
Christ

Christ hath now appeared, like a *Day-starre* with most cheerfull beames; nay, he is the *Sun of Righteousnesse himself*; which hath risen upon the World with his *healing wings*, with his exhilarating light, that he might chase away all those black despairing thoughts from us. But Christ did not rise, that we should play, and sport, and wantonize with his light; but that we should do *the works of the day* in it: that we should walk εὐσχημόνως (as the Apostle speaketh) not in our *Night-clothes* of sinfull Deformity, but clad all over with the comely *Garments of Light*. The Gospel is not big with child of a *Phancie*, of a mere *Conceit* of righteousnesse without us, hanging at distance over us; whilst our hearts within, are nothing but Cages of *unclean birds*, and like Houses continually haunted with Devils, nay the very Rendezvouz of those Fiends of Darknesse. Holinesse, is the best thing, that God himself can bestow upon us, either in this World, or the World to come. True Evangelicall Holinesse, that is, *Christ formed* in the hearts of believers, is the very Cream, and Quintessence of the *Gospel*.

And

And were our hearts found within, were there not many thick and dark fumes, that did arise from thence, and cloud our understandings, we could not easily conceive the substance of Heaven it self, to be any thing else but *Holinesse*, freed from those encumbrances, that did ever clog it, and accloy it here; neither should we wish for any other Heaven, besides this. But many of us are like those Children, whose Stomacks are so vitiated by some disease, that they think, Ashes, Coal, Mudwall, or any such trash, to be more pleasant, then the most wholesome food: such sickly and distempered Appetites have we about these spirituall things, that hanker after I know not what vain shews of happinesse, whilst in the mean time we neglect that which is the onely true food of our souls, that is able solidly to nourish them up to *everlasting life*. Grace is *Holinesse Militant*, Holinesse encumbred with many enemies and difficulties, which it still fights against, and manfully quits it self of: and Glory is nothing else, but *Holinesse Triumphant*; Holinesse with a Palme of Victorie in her hand, and a Crown upon her head. *Deus ipse,*

ipse, cum omni sua bonitate, quatenus extra me est, non facit me beatum; sed quatenus in me est: God himself cannot make me happy, if he be onely without me; and unlesse he give in a participation of himself, and his own likenesse into my soul. Happinesse is nothing, but the releasing and unfettering of our souls, from all these narrow, scant, and particular good things; and the espousing of them to the Highest and most Universall Good, which is not *this* or *that* particular good, but *goodnesse* it self: and this is the same thing that we call Holinesse. Which, because we our selves are so little acquainted with; being for the most part ever courting a mere Shadow of it; therefore we have such low, abject, and beggerly conceits thereof; whereas it is in it self, the most noble, heroicall, and generous thing in the World. For, I mean by Holinesse, nothing else but *God stamped*, & *printed* upon the Soul. And we may please our selves, with what conceits we will; but so long as we are void of this, we do but *dream* of heaven, and, I know not what, fond *Paradise*; we do but blow up and down an *airy Bubble* of our own Phancies, which riseth out of the froth of our vain hearts; we do but court a *painted Heaven*; and woo happinesse in a *Picture*: whilst in the mean time, a *true* and *reall* Hell will suck in our souls into it, and soon make us sensible of a *solid woe*, and *substantiall misery*. Divine wisdome, hath so ordered the frame of the whole Universe, as that every thing should have a certain proper Place, that should be a Receptacle for it. Hell is the Sinke of all sinne and wickednesse. The strong *Magick* of Nature, pulls and draws every thing continually, to that place which is suitable to it, and to which it doth belong: so all these heavy bodies presse downwards, towards the Centre of our earth, being drawn in by it: In like manner Hell wheresoever it is, will by strong *Sympathy* pull in all sinne, and *Magnetically* draw it to it self: as true Holinesse, is always breathing upwards, and fluttering towards Heaven, striving to embosome it self with God: and it will at last undoubtedly be conjoyned with him, no *dismall shades* of darknesse, can possibly stop it in its course, or beat it back;

Ὡς ἀεὶ τὸ ὅμοιον ἄγει θεὸς ὡς τὸ ὅμοιον.

Nay, we do but deceive our selves with names;

names; Hell is nothing but the Orbe of Sinne and Wickednesse, or else that Hemisphear of Darknesse, in which all Evil moves: and Heaven, is the opposite Hemisphear of Light, or else, if you please, the Bright Orbe of Truth, Holinesse, and Goodnesse: and we do actually in this life, instate our selves in the possession of one or other of them. Take Sinne and Disobedience out of Hell, and it will presently clear up, into Light, Tranquillity, Serenity, and shine out into a Heaven. Every true Saint, carrieth his Heaven about with him, in his own heart; and Hell that is without him, can have no power over him. He might safely wade through Hell it self, and like the *Three children*, passe through the midst of that *fiery Furnace*, and yet not at all be scorched with the flames of it: he might walk through the *Valley of the shadow of death*, and yet *fear no evil*. Sinne, is the onely thing in the World, that is contrary to God: God is Light, and that is Darknesse: God is Beauty, and that is Uglinesse and Deformity. All sinne is direct Rebellion against God; and with what Notions soever, we may sugar it, and sweeten it, yet

God can never smile upon it, he will never make a truce with it. God declares open warre againſt ſinne, and bids defiance to it; for it is a profeſſed enemy to Gods own Life and Being. God which is infinite Goodneſſe, cannot but hate ſinne, which is purely Evil. And though ſinne be in it ſelf, but a poore, impotent, and crazy thing, nothing but Straitneſſe, Poverty, and Non-entity; ſo that of it ſelf it is the moſt wretched and miſerable thing in the world, and needeth no further puniſhment beſides it ſelf; yet Divine Vengeance, beats it off ſtill further and further from God, and whereſoever it is, will be ſure to ſcourge it, and laſh it continually. God and Sinne can never agree together.

That, I may therefore come, yet nearer to our ſelves. *This is the Meſſage, that I have now to declare unto you, That God is Light, and in him is no darkneſſe at all: if we ſay that we have Fellowſhip with him, and walke in Darkneſſe, we lie, and do not the truth.* (hriſt, and the *Goſpel* are light, and there is no darkneſſe at all in them; if you *ſay that you know* Chriſt and his Goſpel, & yet *keep not Chriſts Commandments*, but dearly hug, your private darling corruptions; *you are*

are liars, and the truth is not in you; you have no acquaintance with the God of Light, nor the Gospel of Light. If any of you say, that you *know Christ*, and have an interest in him, and yet (as I fear, too many do) still nourish Ambition, Pride, Vainglory within your brests; harbour Malice, Revengfulnesse, & cruell Hatred to your neighbours in your hearts; eagerly scramble after this worldly Pelfe, and make the strength of your parts and endeavours serve that blind *Mammon*, the God of this World; If you wallow and tumble in the filthy puddle of fleshly Pleasures; or if you aime onely at your selves in your lives, and make your *Self* the Compasse by which you sail, and the Starre by which you steer your Course, looking at nothing higher, and more noble then *your selves*; deceive not your selves, *you have neither seen Christ, nor known him*; you are deeply incorporated, (if I may so speak) with the *Spirit of this World*, and have no true *Sympathy* with God and Christ, no *fellowship* at all with them. And (I beseech you) let us consider; Be there not many of us, that pretend much to Christ; that are plainly in our lives, as Proud, Ambitious, Vainglorious as any others? Be there not many of us, that are as much under the power of unruly Passions; as Cruell, Revengefull, Malicious, Censorious as others? that have our minds as deeply engaged in the World, & as much envassalled to Riches, Gain, Profit, those great admired Deities of the sonnes of men, and their souls as much overwhelmed, and sunke with the cares of this life? Do not many of us, as much give our selves to the Pleasures of the flesh, and though not without regrets of Conscience, yet ever now and then secretly soke our selves in them? Be there not many of us that have as deep a share likewise, in Injustice & Oppression, in *vexing the fatherlesse and the widows*? I wish, it may not prove some of our Cases, at that last day, to use such pleas as these unto Christ in our behalfe; *Lord, I have prophecied in thy name*; I have preached many a zealous Sermon for thee; I have kept many a long Fast; I have been very active for thy cause in Church, in State; nay, I never made any question, but that my name was written in thy book of Life; when yet alas, we shall receive no other return from Christ,

Chrift, but this, *I know you not; Depart from me ye Workers of Iniquity.* I am fure, there be too many of us, that have long pretended to Chrift, which make little or no progreffe in *true Chriftianity*, that is, Holineffe of life: that ever hang hovering in a *Twilight of Grace*, and never ferioufly put our felves forwards into clear *Day-light*, but efteem that glimmering *Crepufculum* which we are in, and like that faint *Twilight*, better then broad open Day: whereas, *The Path of the juft* (as the *Wifeman* fpeaketh) *is as the fhining light, that fhineth more and more unto the perfect day.* I am fure, there be many of us, that are perpetuall *Dwarfs* in our fpirituall Stature; like thofe *filly women* (that S. *Paul* fpeaks of) *laden with finnes, and led away with divers lufts, that are ever learning, and never able to come to the knowledge of the truth*: that are not now one jot taller in Chriftianity, then we were many years ago; but have ftill as fickly, crazy, and unfound a temper of foul, as we had long before. Indeed we feem to do fomething, we are alwayes moving and lifting at the ftone of Corruption, that lies upon our hearts, but yet we never ftirre it notwithftanding,

or

or at least never roll it off from us. We are sometimes a little troubled with the guilt of our sinnes, and then we think we must thrust our lusts out of our hearts, but afterwards we sprinkle our selves over, with I know not what *Holy-water*, and so are contented to let them still abide, quietly within us. We do every day truly confesse the same sinnes, and pray against them, and yet still commit them as much as ever, and lie as deeply under the power of them. We have the same Water to pump out in every prayer, and still we let the same, leake in again upon us. We make a great deal of noise, and raise a great deal of dust with our feet; but we do not move from off the ground on which we stood, we do not go forward at all: or if we do sometimes make a little progresse, we quickly loose again, the ground which we had gained: like those upper *Planets* in the Heaven, which (as the *Astronomers* tell us) sometimes move forwards, sometimes quite backwards, and sometimes perfectly stand still; have their *Stations* and *Retrogradations*, as well as their *Direct Motions*. As if Religion were nothing
else,

else, but a *Dancing* up and down, upon the same piece of ground and making severall Motions and Friskings on it; and not a sober Journying, and Travelling onwards toward some certain place. We Doe and Undoe; we do *Penelopes telam texere*, we weave sometimes a *Web of Holinesse*, but then we let our lusts come, and undoe, and unravell all again. Like *Sisyphus* in the Fable, we roll up a mighty Stone with much ado, sweating and tugging up the Hill; and then we let it go, and tumble down again unto the bottome: and this is our constant work. Like those *Danaides* which the *Poets* speak of, we are alwayes filling water into a Sive, by our Prayers, Duties, and Performances; which still runs out as fast as we poure it in. What is it that thus cheats us and gulls us of our Religion? That makes us, thus constantly to tread the same Ring, and Circle of Duties, where we make no progresse at all forwards; and the further we go, are still never the nearer to our journeys end? What is it that thus starves our Religion; and makes it look like those *Kine* in *Pharaohs* Dream, *illfavoured and lean fleshed*;

that

that it hath no Colour in its face, no Bloud in its veines, no Life nor Heat at all, in its members? What is it that doth thus *bedwarfe* us in our Christianity? What low, sordid, and unworthy Principles do we act by, that thus hinder our growth, and make us stand at a stay, and keep us alwayes in the very Porch and Entrance, where we first began? Is it a sleepy, sluggish Conceit, That it is enough for us, if we be but once in a *State of Grace*, if we have but once stepped over the threshold, we need not take so great paines to travel any further? Or is it another damping, choaking, stifling Opinion, That Christ hath done all for us already *without us*, and nothing need more to be done *within* us? No matter, how wicked we be in our selves, for we have holinesse *without us*; no matter, how sickly and diseased our souls be within, for they have health *without them*. Why may we not as well be satisfied, and contented, to have Happinesse without us too to all Eternity, and so our selves forever continue miserable? *Little Children, let no man deceive you: he that doth righteousnesse, is righteous, even as he is righteous*: but, *he that committeth*

committeth sinne is of the Devil. I shall therefore exhort you in the wholesome words of S. Peter; *Give all diligence, to adde to your faith, vertue; and to vertue, knowledge; to knowledge, temperance, and to temperance, patience; to patience, godlinesse; and to godlinesse, brotherly kindnesse; and to brotherly kindnesse, charity; For if these things be in you, and abound, they make you that ye shall neither be barren, nor unfruitfull in the knowledge of our Lord Jesus Christ.* The Apostle still goes on, and I cannot leave him yet; *But he that lacketh these things is blind, and cannot see far off, and hath forgotten that he was once purged from his old sinnes. Wherefore the rather Brethren, give diligence to make your calling and election sure: for if ye do these things, ye shall never fall.* Let us not onely talk and dispute of Christ, but let us indeed *put on the Lord Jesus Christ.* Having those *great and precious promises,* which he hath given us, let us strive to be made *partakers of the Divine Nature, escaping the corruption that is in the world through lust*: and being begotten again to a *lively hope* of enjoying Christ hereafter, *let us purifie our selves as he is pure.* Let us really declare, that we *know Christ,* that we are his Disciples, by

our

our *keeping of his Commandments* : and amongst the rest, that *Commandment* especially which our Saviour Christ himself commendeth to his Disciples in a peculiar manner; *This is my commandment, That ye love one another, as I have loved you:* and again; *These things I command you, that you love one another. Let us follow peace with all men, and holinesse, without which, no man shall see God. Let us put on as the Elect of God, holy, and beloved, bowels of mercies, kindnesse, humblenesse of mind, meeknesse, longsuffering, forbearing one another, and forgiving one another, if any man have a quarel against any, even as Christ forgave us: And above all these things let us put on Charity, which is the bond of perfectnesse. Let us in meeknesse, instruct those that oppose themselves, if God peradventure will give them repentance, to the acknowledging of the truth, that they may recover themselves out of the snares of the Devil, that are taken captive by him at his will. Beloved, Let us love another, for Love is of God, and whosoever loveth is born of God and knoweth God.* O Divine Love! the sweet Harmony of souls! the Musick of Angels! The Joy of Gods own Heart, the very Darling of his Bosome! the Sourse of true Happinesse! the

pure

pure Quintessence of Heaven! That which reconciles the jarring Principles of the World, and makes them all chime together! That which melts mens Hearts into one another! see how S. *Paul* describes it, and it cannot choose but enamour your affections towards it: *Love envieth not, it is not puffed up, it doth not behave it self unseemly, seeketh not her own, is not easily provoked, thinketh no evil, rejoyceth not in iniquity; beareth all things, believeth all things, hopeth all things, endureth all things:* I may adde in a word, it is the best natur'd thing, the best complexioned thing, in the World. Let us expresse this sweet harmonious Affection, in these jarring times: that so if it be possible, we may tune the World at last, into better Musick. Especially, in matters of Religion, let us strive with all meeknesse to instruct and convince one another. Let us endeavour to promote the *Gospel of Peace*, the *Dove-like Gospel* with a *Dove-like Spirit*. This was the way by which the Gospel at first, was propagated in the world: *Christ did not cry, nor lift up his voice in the streets, a bruised reed he did not break, and the smoking flax he did not quench*

and yet he brought forth judgement into victory. He whispered the Gospel to us from Mount *Sion*, in a still voice, and yet the sound thereof went out quickly throughout all the earth. The Gospel at first came down upon the world gently and softly, like the *Dew* upon *Gideons fleece*, and yet it quickly soaked quite through it : and doubtlesse this is still the most effectuall way to promote it further. Sweetnesse, and Ingenuity , will more powerfully command mens minds , then Passion, Sowrenesse, and Severity : as the soft Pillow sooner breaks the Flint, then the hardest Marble. Let us ἀληθεύϊν ἐν ἀγάπῃ, *follow truth in love* : and of the two indeed, be contented rather, to misse of the conveying of a Speculative Truth, then to part with Love. When we would convince men of any errour by the strength of *Truth*, let us withall poure the sweet Balme of Love upon their heads. *Truth* and *Love* , are two the most powerfull things in the world, and when they both go together , they cannot easily be withstood. The Golden Beams of Truth, and the Silken Cords of Love, twisted together , will draw men on with a
sweet

sweet violence, whether they will or no. Let us take heed we do not sometimes call that Zeal for God, and his Gospel, which is nothing else, but our own tempestuous and stormy Passion. True Zeal is a sweet, heavenly and gentle Flame, which maketh us active for God, but always within the Sphear of Love. It never calls for *Fire from Heaven*, to consume those that differ a little from us in their Apprehensions. It is like that kind of Lightning, (which the Philosophers speak of) that melts the Sword within, but singeth not the Scabbard: it strives to save the Soul, but hurteth not the Body. True Zeal is a loving thing, and makes us always active to *Edification*, and not to *Destruction*. If we keep the Fire of Zeal within the Chimney, in its own proper place, it never doth any hurt; it onely warmeth, quickeneth, and enliveneth us: but if once we let it break out, and catch hold of the Thatch of our Flesh, and kindle our corrupt Nature, and set the House of our Body on fire, it is no longer Zeal, it is no heavenly Fire, it is a most destructive and devouring thing. True Zeal is an *Ignis lambens*

bens, a soft and gentle Flame, that will not scorch ones hand; it is no predatory or voracious thing: but *Carnall and fleshly Zeal*, is like the Spirit of Gunpowder set on fire, that tears and blows up all that stands before it. True Zeal is like the *Vitall heat* in us, that we live upon, which we never feel to be angry or troublesome; but though it gently feed upon the *Radicall Oyl* within us, that sweet Balsame of our *Naturall Moisture*; yet it lives lovingly with it, and maintains that by which it is fed: but that other furious & distempered Zeal, is nothing but a *Feaver* in the Soul. To conclude, we may learn what kind of Zeal it is, that we should make use of in promoting the Gospel, by an Emblem of Gods own, given us in the Scripture, those *Fiery Tongues* that upon the Day of *Pentecost*, sate upon the Apostles; which sure were harmlesse Flames, for we cannot reade that they did any hurt, or that they did so much as singe an haire of their heads. I will therefore shut up this, with that of the *Apostle*: *Let us keep the unity of the Spirit in the bond of peace.* Let this soft and silken Knot of *Love*, tie our Hearts together;
though

though our Heads and Apprehenſions cannot meet, as indeed they never will, but alwayes ſtand at ſome diſtance off from one another. Our Zeal if it be heavenly, if it be true *Veſtall Fire* kindled from above, it will not delight to tarry here below, burning up Straw and Stubble, and ſuch combuſtible things, and ſending up nothing but groſſe earthy fumes to heaven; but it will riſe up, and return back, pure as it came down, and will be ever ſtriving to carry up mens hearts to God along with it. It will be onely occupied, about the promoting of thoſe things, which are *unqueſtionably good* ; and when it moves in the iraſcible way, it will quarrel with nothing but *ſinne*. Here let our zeal buſie and exerciſe it ſelf, every one of us beginning firſt at our own hearts. Let us be more Zealous then ever we have yet been, in fighting againſt our luſts, in pulling down thoſe *ſtrong holds of Sinne and Satan* in our hearts. Here let us exerciſe all our Courage and Reſolution, our Manhood and Magnanimitie. Let us truſt in the *Almighty Arme* of our God, and doubt not, but he will as well deliver us, from the *Power of*

K   *Sinne*

Sinne in our hearts, as preferve us from the *wrath to come*. Let us go out againſt theſe *uncircumciſed Philiſtines*, I mean our Luſts, not with *Shield or Spear*, not in any confidence of our own ſtrength, but in the name of the *Lord of Hoſts*, and we ſhall prevail: we ſhall overcome our Luſts, *for greater is he that is in us, then he that is in them. The Eternall God is our refuge, and underneath are the everlaſting arms: He ſhall thruſt out theſe enemies from before us, and he ſhall ſay, Deſtroy them.* We ſhall enter the *true Canaan*, the good Land of Promiſe, *that floweth with milk and honey*, the Land of Truth and Holineſſe. *Wherefore take unto you the whole armour of God, that you may be able to withſtand: let your loines be girt about with truth; have on the breſtplate of righteouſneſſe; and let your feet be ſhod with the preparation of the Goſpel of peace. Above all take the ſhield of faith, whereby you ſhall be able to quench all the fiery darts of the Wicked, and take the helmet of ſalvation, and the ſword of the ſpirit, which is the word of God.* And laſtly, be ſure of this, That ye *be ſtrong onely in the Lord*, and *in the power of his might*. There be ſome that diſhearten us in this ſpirituall warfare, and would make
us

us let our weapons fall out of our hands, by working in us a defpair of Victory. There be fome *evil Spies*, that *weaken* the hands and the hearts of the *children* of *Ifrael*: and bring an ill report upon that land that we are to conquer, telling of nothing but ftrange *Gyants*, the *fonnes of Anak* there, that we fhall never be able to overcome. *The Amalekites*, (fay they) *dwell in the South, the Hittites, Jebufites, Amorites in the Mountains, and the Canaanites by the Sea-coaft*: huge armies of tall invincible *Lufts*: *we fhall never be able to go againft this people*, we fhall never be able to prevail againft our *Corruptions*. Hearken not unto them (I befeech you) but hear what *Caleb* and *Jofhuah* fay; *Let us go up at once, and poffeffe it, for we are able to overcome them*: not by our own ftrength, but by the power of the *Lord of Hofts*. There are indeed *Sonnes of Anak* there, there are mighty *Gyantlike Lufts*, that we are to graple with; nay there are, *Principalities*, and *Powers* too, that we are to oppofe: but the great *Michael, the Captain of the Lords Hoft* is with us; he commands in chief for us, and we need not be difmayed. *Underftand therefore this day,*

K 2   That

That the Lord thy God is he, which goeth before thee, as a consuming fire, he shall destroy these *enemies, and bring them down before thy face.* If thou wilt be faithfull to him, and put thy trust in him ; *as the fire consumeth the stubble, and as the flame burneth up the chaff,* so will he destroy thy *Lusts* in thee : *their root shall be rottennesse, and their blossome shall go up as dust.* But let us take heed that we be not discouraged, and before we begin to fight, despair of Victorie : but to believe and hope well in the power of our God and his strength, will be half a Conquest. Let us not think, Holinesse in the hearts of men here in the World, is a forlorn, forsaken, and outcast thing from God ; that he hath no regard of. Holinesse where-ever it is, though never so small, if it be but hearty and sincere, it can no more be cut off, and discontinued from God ; then a *Sun-beam* here upon Earth can be broken off, from its entercourse with the *Sun*, and be left alone amidst the mire and dirt of this World. The Sun may as well discard its own *Rayes*, and banish them from it self, into some Region of darknesse, far remote from it, where they

shall

shall have no dependence at all upon it, as God can forsake and abandon Holinesse in the World, and leave it a poore Orphane thing, that shall have no influence at all from him to preserve and keep it. Holinesse is something of God, where-ever it is; it is an *Efflux* from him, that alwayes hangs upon him, and lives in him: as the *Sun-beams* though they guild this lower World, and spread their golden wings over us; yet they are not so much here, where they shine, as in the Sun, from whence they flow. God cannot draw a Curtain betwixt himself and Holinesse, which is nothing, but the *Splendor* and *Shining* of himself: He cannot hide his face from it, he cannot desert it, in the World. He that is once *born of God, shall overcome the World*, and the Prince of this World too, by the Power of God in him. Holinesse is no solitary neglected thing; it hath stronger Confederacies, greater Alliances then Sinne and Wickednesse. It is in league with God, and the whole Universe; the whole Creation smiles upon it: there is something of God in it, and therefore it must needs be, a victorious and triumphant thing.

thing. Wickednesse is a weak, cowardly, and guilty thing, a fearfull and trembling Shadow. It is the Child of Ignorance and Darknesse; it is afraid of Light, and cannot possibly withstand the power of it, nor endure the sight of its glittering Armour. It is allianced to none, but wretched forlorn and apostate Spirits, that do what they can, to support their own weak and tottering Kingdome of Darknesse: but are onely strong, in Weaknesse and Impotency. The whole Politie and Commonwealth of Devils, is not so powerfull, as one *Child of Light*, one *Babe in Christ*: they are not all able to *quench* the least *smoking flax*, to exstinguish one spark of Grace. Darknesse is not able to make resistance against Light, but ever as it comes, flies before it. But if wickednesse, invite the Society of Devils to it, (as we learn by the sad experience of these present times, in many examples of those that were possessed with Malice, Revengfulnesse, and Lust) so that those cursed Fiends do most readily apply themselves to it, and offer their service to feed it and encourage it; because it is their own Life and Nature,

their

their own *kingdome of Darknesse*, which they strive to enlarge, and to spread the Dominions of: shall we then think that Holinesse, which is so nearly allied unto God, hath no good *Genius* at all in the World, to attend upon it, to help it and encourage it? Shall not the *Kingdome of Light*, be as true to its own Interest, and as vigilant for the enlarging of it self, as the *Kingdome of Darknesse*? Holinesse is never alone in the World, but God is alwayes with it, and his loving *Spirit*, doth ever associate, and joyn it self to it. He that sent it into the World, is with it, as Christ speaketh of himself, *the Father hath not left me alone, because I do alwayes those things that please him.* Holinesse is the Life of God, which he cannot but feed and maintain wheresoever it is; and as the Devils are alwayes active to encourage evil, so we cannot imagine, but that the heavenly Host of blessed Angels above, are as busily employed, in the promoting of that which they love best, that which is dearest to God whom they serve, the *Life* and *Nature of God*. *There is joy in heaven at the conversion of one sinner,* Heaven takes notice of it; there is a *Quire of* of Angels that sweetly sings the *Epithalamium* of a Soul divorced from Sinne and Satan, and espoused unto Christ. What therefore the *Wiseman* speaks concerning *Wisdome*, I shall apply to *Holinesse*: *Take fast hold of Holinesse, let her not go, keep her for she is thy Life* : *Keep thy heart with all diligence for out of it are the issues of Life,* & of Death too. Let nothing be esteemed, of greater consequence and concernment to thee, then what thou doest and acteſt, how thou liveſt. Nothing *without* us can make us either happy, or miserable ; nothing can either *defile us*, or hurt us, but what *goeth out from us*, what Springeth and Bubbleth up, out of our own hearts. We have dreadfull apprehensions, of the Flames of Hell without us ; we tremble and are afraid, when we hear of *Fire and Brimstone*, whil'ſt in the mean time, we securely nourish within our own hearts, *a true and living Hell,*

——— *Et cæco carpimur igni :*

the dark fire of our Luſts, consumeth our bowels within, and miserably scorcheth our souls, and we are not troubled at it. We do not perceive, how Hell ſteales upon us, whileſt we live here. And as for Heaven, we we onely gaze abroad, expecting that it should come in to us from without, but never look for the beginnings of it to arise within, in our own hearts.

But left there should yet happely remain any prejudice against that, which I have all this while heartily commended to you; *True Holinesse*, and the *Keeping of Christs commandment*; as if it were a *Legall* and *Servile* thing, that would subject us to a *State* of *Bondage*, I must here needs adde a Word or two, either for the Prevention or Removall of it. I do not therefore mean, by *Holinesse*, the mere performance of outward Duties of Religion, coldly acted over as a task, not our habituall Prayings, Hearings, Fastings, multiplied one upon another (though these be all good, as subservient to an higher end) but I mean an inward *Soul* and *Principle* of *Divine Life*, that spiriteth all these; that enliveneth and quickeneth, the dead carkasse, of all our outward Performances whatsoever. I do not here urge, the *dead Law of outward Works*, which indeed if it be alone, subjects us to a *State of Bondage*; but the *inward Law* of the Gospel, the *Law of the Spirit of Life*, then which nothing can be more free and ingenuous: for it doth not act us by Principles without us, but is an inward *Self-moving* Principle, living in our Hearts. I do not urge the Law written upon *Tables of stone* without us (though there is still a good use of that too) but the Law of Holinesse written within, upon the *Fleshly Tables of our hearts*. The first, though it work us into some outward Conformity to Gods Commandments, and so hath a good effect upon the World; yet we are all this while, but like dead Instruments of Musick, that sound sweetly and harmoniously, when they are onely struck, and played upon from without, by the Musicians Hand, who hath the Theory and *Law* of Musick, *living* within himself. But the Second, the *living* Law of the Gospel, the *Law of the Spirit of Life* within us, is as if the *Soul of Musick*, should incorporate it self with the Instrument, and live in the Strings, and make them of their own accord, without any touch, or impulse from without, daunce up and down, and warble out their Harmonies. They that are

acted

acted onely by an outward Law, are but like Neurospasts, or those little Puppets that skip nimbly up and down, and seem to be full of quick and sprightly motion, whereas they are all the while moved artificially by certain Wiers and Strings from without, and not by any Principle of Motion, from themselves within: or else, like Clocks and Watches, that go pretty regularly for a while, but are moved by Weights and Plummets, or some other Artificiall Springs, that must be ever now and then wound up, or else they cease. But they that are acted by the *new Law of the Gospel*, by the *Law of the Spirit*, they have an inward principle of life in them, that from the Centre of it self, puts forth it self freely and constantly into all obedience to the will of Christ. This *New Law of the Gospel*, it is a kind of *Musicall Soul*, informing the dead *Organ* of our Hearts, that makes them of their own accord delight to act harmoniously according to the Rule of Gods word. The Law that I speak of, it is a *Law of Love*, which is the most powerfull Law in the World; and yet it freeth us in a manner from all Law without us, us, because it maketh us become a *Law unto our selves*. The more it prevaileth in us, the more it eateth up and devoureth, all other Laws without us; just as Aarons *Living Rod*, did swallow up those Rods of the Magicians, that were made onely to counterfeit a little Life:

Quis Legem det amantibus?
Major lex Amor est sibi.

Love is at once a Freedome from all Law, a State of purest Liberty, and yet a Law too, of the most constraining and indispensable Necessity. The worst *Law* in the World, is *the Law of Sinne, which is in our members*; which keeps us in a condition of most absolute Slavery, when we are wholy under the Tyrannicall commands of our lusts: this is a cruell *Pharaoh* indeed, that sets his hard task-masters over us, and maketh us wretchedly drudge in Mire and Clay. The *Law of the Letter* without us, sets us in a condition of a little more Liberty, by restraining of us from many outward Acts of Sinne; but yet it doth not disenthrall us, from the power of sinne in our hearts. But the *Law of the Spirit of life*, the *Gospel-Law of Love*,

Love, it puts us into a condition of most pure and perfect Liberty; and whosoever really entertaines this Law, he hath *thrust out Hagar* quite, he hath *cast out the Bondwoman and her Children*; from henceforth, *Sarah the Free woman*, shall live forever with him, and she shall be to him, a Mother of many children; her seed shall be *as the sand of the sea-shoar for number*, and *as the starres of heaven*. Here is Evangelicall liberty, here is Gospel-freedome, when *the Law of the Spirit of life in Christ Jesus, hath made us free, from the Law of sinne and death*: when we have a liberty from sinne, and not a liberty to sinne: for our dear Lord and Master hath told us, that *Whosoever committeth sinne, he is the servant of it*. He that lies under the power, and vassallage of his base lusts, and yet talks of Gospel-freedome; he is but like a poore condemned Prisoner, that in his sleep dreams of being set at liberty, and of walking up and down wheresoever he pleaseth; whilst his Legs are all the while lock't fast in fetters and Irons. To please our selves with a Notion of Gospel-liberty, whilest we have not a Gospel-principle of Holinesse within us, us, to free us from the power of sinne, it is nothing else, but to gild over our Bonds and Fetters, and to phancy our selves to be in a Golden Cage. There is a Straitnesse, Slavery, and Narrownesse in all Sinne: Sinne crowds and crumples up our souls, which if they were freely spread abroad, would be as wide, and as large as the whole Universe. No man is truly free, but he that hath his *will* enlarged to the extent of Gods own will, by loving whatsoever God loves, and nothing else. Such a one, doth not fondly hug this and that particular created good thing, and envassal himself unto it, but he loveth every thing that is lovely, beginning at God, and descending down to all his Creatures, according to the severall degrees of perfection in them. He injoyes a boundlesse Liberty, and a boundlesse Sweetnesse, according to his boundlesse Love. He inclaspeth the whole World within his outstretched arms, his Soul is as wide as the whole Universe, as big as *yesterday, to day, and forever*. Whosoever is once acquainted with this Disposition of Spirit, he never desires any thing else: and he loves the *Life of of God* in himself, dearer then his own Life. To conclude this therefore ; If we love Christ, and *keep his commandments, his commandments will not be grievous to us: His yoke will be easie, and his burden light*: it will not put us into a State of Bondage, but of perfect Liberty. For it is most true of Evangelicall Obedience, what the wise man speaketh of Wisdome ; *Her wayes, are wayes of pleasantnesse, and all her paths are peace ; She is a tree of Life to those that lay hold upon her, and happy are all they that retain her.*

I will now shut up all with one or two *Considerations* to perswade you further, to the *keeping of Christs Commandments*.

First, from the desire which we all have of *Knowledge* ; If we would indeed *know* Divine Truths, the onely way to come to this, is by *keeping of Christs Commandments*. The Grossenesse of our apprehensions in *Spirituall things*, and our many mistakes, that we have about them, proceed from nothing, but those dull and foggy *Stemes*, which rise up from our *foul hearts* and becloud our Understandings. If we did but

heartily

heartily comply with Chrifts commandments, and purge our hearts, from all groffe and fenfuall affections, we fhould not then look about for *Truth* wholly without our felves, and enflave our felves to the Dictates of this and that Teacher, and hang upon the *Lips of men*; but we fhould find the Great Eternall God, inwardly teaching our fouls, and continually inftructing us more and more, in the myfteries of his will: and *out of our bellies fhould flow rivers of living waters.* Nothing puts a ftop and hinderance to the paffage of Truth in the World, but the Carnality of our hearts, the Corruption of our lives. 'Tis not wrangling Difputes and Syllogifticall Reafonings, that are the mighty Pillars, that underprop *Truth* in the World; if we would but underfet it with the Holineffe of our Hearts and Lives, it fhould never fail. *Truth* is a prevailing and conquering thing, and would quickly overcome the World, did not the Earthineffe of our Difpofitions, and the Darkneffe of our falfe hearts hinder it. Our Saviour Chrift, bids the *Blind man*, wafh off the *Clay* that was upon his eyes, in the *Pool of Siloam*, and then

then he should see clearly; intimating this to us, that it is the Earthinesse of mens Affections, that darkens the Eye of their understandings in Spirituall things. Truth is alwayes ready, and near at hand, if our eyes were not closed up with Mud, that we could but open them, to look upon it. Truth, always waits upon our souls, and offers it self freely to us, as the Sun offers its beams, to every Eye, that will but open, and let them shine in upon it. If we could but purge our Hearts, from that filth, and defilement, which hangeth about them, there would be no doubt at all of *Truths* prevailing in the World. For, *Truth is great, and stronger then all things; all the Earth calleth upon Truth, and the heaven blesseth it, all works shake and tremble at it. The Truth endureth, and is alwayes strong, it liveth and conquereth for evermore. She is the Strength, Kingdome, Power and Majestie of all ages. Blessed be the God of Truth.*

Last of all, if we desire a true Reformation, as we seem to do; Let us begin here in reforming our *hearts* and *lives* ; in *keeping of Chrifts Commandments.* All outward Formes and Models of Reformation, though they be

never

never so good in their kind; yet they are of little worth to us, without this *inward Reformation of* the heart. Tinne, or Lead, or any other baser Metal, if it be cast into never so good a Mold, and made up into never so elegant a Figure; yet it is but Tin, or Lead still, it is the same Metal, that it was before. And if we be Molded into never so good a Form of outward Government, unlesse we *new mold our Hearts* within too; we are but a little better, then we were before. If adulterate Silver, that hath much Allay or Drosse in it, have never so current a Stamp put upon it, yet it will not passe notwithstanding, when the Touch-stone trieth it. We must be *reformed within*, with a *Spirit* of *Fire*, and a *Spirit of Burning*, to purge us from the Drosse, and Corruption of our hearts; and refine us as Gold and Silver; and then we shall be *reformed truly*, and not before. When this once comes to passe, then shall Christ be set *upon his Throne* indeed, then the Glory *of the Lord shall overflow the Land*; then we shall be a People acceptable unto him, and as *Mount Sion,* which he dearly loved.

FINIS.

Die Mercurii ultimo Martii. 1647.

ORdered by the Commons assembled in Parliament: That Sr Henry Mildmay, *do from this House give thanks unto* Mr *Cudworth, for the great paines he took, in the Sermon he preached on this day at Margarets* Westminster, *before the House of Commons (it being a day of Publick Humiliation) and that he do desire him to print his Sermon. Wherein he is to have the like Priviledge in printing thereof, as others in like kind usually have had.*

                      H. Elsynge,
                      Cler. Parl. D. Com.

Bei Fragen zur Produktsicherheit wenden Sie sich bitte an:
If you have any questions regarding product safety,
please contact:

Walter de Gruyter GmbH
Genthiner Straße 13
10785 Berlin
productsafety@degruyterbrill.com